THE FOOD MONOLOGUES

by KERRI KOCHANSKI

SPECIAL NOTE

Cover Image: moni158/deviantart

THE FOOD
MONOLOGUES

THE FOOD MONOLOGUES was produced as a one-act play by Emerging Artists Theatre (NYC, April 2008). It was directed by Deb Guston. The cast was as follows:

FELICIA . . . . .Sarah Schmitz

RENEE .Sarah Miriam Aziz

SUZANNE . . . . .Janelle M. Lannan

TARA . . . . .Elizabeth Gwynne Wilson

KERTIE . . . . Erin Hadley

SYLVIE . . . . .Kelly Dynan

JESS . . . . .Rhonda Ayers

KELLI . . . . Michele Fulves

SHERRY . . . . Alexandra Zabriskie

FRIEDA . . . . .Andrea Alton

CHLOE .Stephanie Deliani

JENNY . . . . Laine Buntrock

REBECCA . . . . Randi Sobol

The play has been expanded into this full-length play.

Monologues from the play are published in the following anthologies: Young Women's Monologues from Contemporary Plays (Meriwether, 2004), Audition Arsenal for Women in Their 30's (Smith & Kraus, 2005), and Young Women's Monologues from Contemporary Plays: Volume II (Meriwether, 2008).

CHARACTERS.

FELICIA/DEVIL	20s. College student. A purger with body dysmorphic disorder. A healthy thin.
RENEE/ONE/SNAKE	20s. An exercise bulimic. Toned.
SUZANNE/HEAD	30s. Newlywed. A binger.
TARA/TWO/HOWARD STERN/YOUNG SHERRY	20s. Beautiful. Perfect body. A sploshee.
KERTIE/THREE/EVE	30s. Pretty, sexy. A secret eater. Chunky.
SYLVIE/HEAD	20s. Hesitant. Pregnant.
JESS/FOUR/HEAD	30s. An eater. Appears confident. 2nd largest.
KELLI/FIVE	30s. Wife/mother. A restrictive eater.
SHERRY/SIX/ HUGH HEFNER	40s. Dowdy housewife. Downtrodden.
FRIEDA/SEVEN/ DEVIL	30s. Harried mom. A Coca-Cola addict.
CHLOE/EIGHT	30s. Live-in girlfriend. A calorie prisoner.
JENNY/NINE/CHILD DONALD TRUMP	Teens. Student. An anorexic chew & spitter. Extremely thin.
REBECCA/HEAD	30s. Depressed. Extremely obese.
AUDIENCE MEMBER	Doubling, or played by plant/crew.
AUDIENCE MEMBER #2	Doubling, or played by plant/crew.

NOTE.
ONE through NINE function as a CHORUS. They wear black shirts, and black pants/skirts.

TIME & PLACE.
Now, America

RUNNING TIME.
100 minutes.

SET.
There is a minimal set:

4 screens (for slide titles, video images and text)

A black wall or black curtain, which has cutouts for heads

A large gray curtain, which is bunched up into the shape of a Mound

(*The Mound is present throughout the play. It does not need to appear in every scene. It is obvious that there is something significant concealed under the Mound. **Note:** The characters do not acknowledge the Mound.*)

TECHNICAL REQUIREMENTS.

The slide title appears in **BOLD**. It is visible on a screen.

The play also features a very short video, or suitable alternative.

LIGHTING.

For monologues (DIM)

For ensemble scenes (BLUE)

For **I Don't Feel Good** (HOUSE LIGHTS)

For **Apple, Peaches, Pumpkin Pie** (PINK)

SOUNDS.

A snake hiss

The cry of a newborn

A director's slate

A ticking clock

NOTES.

(ACT II. Scene 1.) can be performed live, via video, or live with video.

Also, the apple, the salad, and SUZANNE's pile of food should be absurdly gigantic.

THE FOOD
MONOLOGUES

PROLOGUE.

(Before the performance, the audience is offered a slice of chocolate cake and a small drink. They can eat it or not eat it. It is up to them.)

ACT I.

(*The screen reads:*)

THE FOOD MONOLOGUES

(*Lights fade.*)

Scene 1: **ELEPHANT.**

(*Lights rise on Felicia.*)

FELICIA: She scares me…'Cause I was trying to walk past her,
you know – and I just couldn't – I just couldn't get around…It's like
I would try to walk this way. And then I would try to step that
way…Every time…Every *single* time…Like an Elephant.

And it's not like I would tell her to go on a diet. Lord knows, I
would never talk anyone into going on a diet. Unless they wanted to.
Unless they were…"committed…"

(*Lights rise on Mound.*)

Some people spend time, fighting the meal plan…Some people
spend inordinate amounts of time – Like me…Wondering how I can
eat enough of something healthy…Just so I can have enough –
Enough leeway…to eat something…fulfilling…Something
good…Some *thing*…that will click the switch on in my brain that
says "yes" you are happy…Because you are so perfect…So
infallible…You are able to eat whatever you want – and not have to
pay. Pay the price. Em*body* the price…(*Looks down at herself.*) By
showing your body…By revealing your stomach…The stomach that
shows through your everyday pants – not club-hopping pants. Not
tight fitting pants like that. I could wear them once, but I can't wear
them now – I sure as hell can't wear them now – I can't even wear
regular pants. (*Beat.*) And yet this Elephant…

(*Tries to maneuver around elephant.*)

I can't – Get around her.

I would think that would somehow make me feel better – but it
doesn't…It doesn't…

Not when I feel like – Not when I seem like – This elephant
myself…

(*Crossfade.*)

5

Scene 2: **TEN POUNDS.**

> (*Renee jogs.*)

RENEE: *Ten* pounds. I need to lose *ten* pounds…Well, I don't need to really…But I would "like" to…I would "like" to lose ten pounds…"Liking" to and "needing" to are different things. If you would "like" to, then it is something you would "like" to do… Things like fishing or ice skating – Things that you always seem to think about, year after year, but never get around to.

> (*Grows serious.*)

"Needing," though…Some people need to do things…Like filling out taxes…Tax forms, I mean…I don't need to do it…so I don't know…I mean, I need to do it…But my boyfriend does it for me…Some things you need to do, but you can get other people – (*Stops.*) Not weight loss, though…

> (*She begins to quote.*)

'You need to lose weight yourself…' *For* yourself…Not for anybody else…Well, maybe your doctor…If you needed to…But then you would have a purpose, you see…? Heart attack, or diet. Diabetes, or diet.

People that don't need, have less motivation…

> (*Notices weight. Grabs it.*)

This weight…This weight weighs *ten* pounds…*Ten* pounds of fat…that is on my body…And doesn't have to be…If I could just get rid of it –

> (*Considers. Then throws weight to side, resumes jogging.*)

But I don't "need" to…I *want* to…I really, really *want* to…But I don't need to… (*Suddenly, she isn't so sure.*) Do I?

> (*Crossfade.*)

6

Scene 3: **FOUND.**

> (*An enormous pile of food. Suzanne pops out of it, caught. She doesn't know what to do.*)

SUZANNE: You look stumped like…you don't know what's going on. And I don't either. I mean, if I did, I would tell you…I mean, why this crab is in my pocket –

> (*Pulls out crab.*)

Why I have mustard on my lips –

> (*Wipes her lips.*)

And "cookies…" Let's not forget about the "cookies…"

The cookies that were sitting there in the back of the closet for *ten months…Ten months*, Honey…And when I was looking for my coat I saw – Saw because – I don't know – I *wanted* to see. It was *time* to see. Time to see that by hiding the cookies in the closet…By hiding the crabs and the cakes –

Cake…

> (*Takes out piece of wedding cake.*)

Yes, "cake…" And it's not because it's my anniversary. It's because it's cake – And I'm *hungry*…And I don't care if the cake topper is lonely.

> (*Tosses topper.*)

I want to eat it…And cookies and crabs…And whatever else you've got hidden away in there – in the *back* of the closet, in the *back* of the refrigerator. It's my refrigerator, too. I should get to *see* to *see* things.

The wedding's over…

> (*Plops wedding veil on head.*)

7

SUZANNE (cont'd): So I really don't have to be skinny anymore, you know? I really don't need to be skinny.

>*(Doesn't know what to do. Notices crab.)*

Crabs won't make me fat…And they'll be there. Be my friend… when I don't have a friend.

Because cake is no friend. Cookies –

They are food, Honey. They are food…

And I *want* them…I *need* them…I *found* them…

Found them…Before I found you.

>*(Crossfade.)*

Scene 4: **FOOD ISN'T JUST FOR EATING.**

TARA: Food isn't just for eating. It's for wearing. I wear food.
Todd likes me to wear food. Todd likes me to wear food when I am
wearing nothing at all. (*Massages body, runs hands through hair.*)
Todd licks the food. Smells the food. Runs his fingers through the
food and flicks the food with his tongue. He is a food-o-phile…Only
he's only a food-o-phile with *me*. We have a relationship…We can
do these sorts of things…

People in non-committed relationships…I don't know if they can *do*
these sorts of things…Well, they can…Well, they do it with
whipped cream. And pudding. And things like that, I imagine.

>   (*She is suddenly freaked out.*)

But gravy…!? Mashed potatoes…!?

SPLOSHING.

Todd *likes* these sorts of things…And I really wouldn't subject
myself – But he says that he loves me…And doesn't love mean
doing some stuff for other people…!? Doesn't love mean –
Slathering yourself – When really you'd rather you did not. You did
not want to make yourself – A human plate. A human dish. A dish
upon which to dribble food – making it *dirty*. Making it *stink*.
Making it *reek* – Of sardines and sauerkraut –

These are the *other* things…The *other* things…he adds…And it
wouldn't be so bad if I liked them, too…But I don't – And I don't
know if – I can continue –

I just want to *eat*…I want to *eat* food.

Don't you…? *Don't **you**…?*

>   (*Crossfade.*)

9

Scene 5: **REDDIWHIP.**

KERTIE: Food isn't just for eating, like she said...(*Indicates Tara.*) Sometimes you can wear it...Wear food – I wear it for my boyfriend...In front of him...Well, *for* him...He doesn't wear it for me. Too...sticky...But he likes the way it tastes...

> (*She points out.*)

I don't taste it...*He* tastes it...If he put his finger in my mouth, I would lick it – But I wouldn't swallow...It's not for *me*...It's for *him*.

So you see, that's why I do it...

> (*Takes out Reddiwhip. Begins to spray it on body.*)

Other stuff could be done, too...Chocolate pudding, cherries...But I keep it simple...I keep it clean...Wouldn't want to mess it up... Mess him up – Mess me – Mess it – (*Grows embarrassed, flustered.*) Because he likes it – You see...? Because otherwise – Why would I stand here...

> (*She stands there, covered in whipped cream.*)

AUDIENCE MEMBER: DOES IT ITCH...?

KERTIE: It doesn't itch...No, it doesn't itch...But when I have no clothes, it covers – The cellulite, the stretch marks...

> (*Considers.*)

And I think that's why – I think maybe I – Need to think about... Need to wonder about...Why...? Why am I doing – What I don't *want* to be doing...

> (*She suddenly grows indignant.*)

He should eat *me*...Or nothing at all!

> (*Crossfade.*)

10

Scene 6: **I EAT BECAUSE.**

NINE: I eat because my brain tells me to eat.

SIX: Because my heart is broken.

FOUR: Because I broke my leg, and I can't do anything but watch TV, and sometimes, when I get bored of watching TV, I need to do something else. And so I eat! –

EIGHT: – because when I watch TV. I *have* to eat.

SEVEN: Because I have to eat every hour. *On* the hour. (*Afterthought.*) Because I have OCD.

FIVE: Because if I didn't eat, I'd smoke.

NINE: Because food feels good.

SIX: Because it "looks" good. Because they've presented it nicely. On the plate. At the restaurant…And so I figured why not try it? Some of

FOUR: His food

FIVE: Her food

SEVEN: The *kids'* food. They waste it…The kids…And I *paid* for it –

EIGHT: – sometimes, I buy food…And I put it in my glove compartment…Just in case.

SIX: Just in case there is a storm.

FOUR: Or a breakdown.

EIGHT: And I am stranded…But I never get stranded…

NINE: Still I

11

SEVEN: Buy the food.

FIVE: Eat the food.

SEVEN: Eat the food.

FIVE: Buy the food.

FOUR: I put it in my pocket.

NINE: My gym bag…For a quick boost.

SEVEN: Only on Fridays.

FIVE: On Saturdays.

EIGHT: On my birthday –

NINE: – Valentine's Day.

FOUR: During the holidays –

SEVEN: – on holy days. (*Beat.*) I have to fast…So I make up for it.

NINE: I make allowances.

FIVE: Concessions.

NINE: If I'm having a bad day

EIGHT: For example

FIVE: If I got a promotion.

FOUR: Or a raise.

SEVEN: Or lost a pound –

> (*They stop. Four, Nine and Five are disgusted with Seven.*)

FIVE: I've got to get back to work.

NINE: To school.

FOUR: Excuse me, I have to go.

EIGHT: To the gym!

> (*They rush off.*
>
> *Sylvie enters. Eight notices Sylvie's stomach. She gives it a dirty look.*
>
> *Crossfade.*)

Scene 7: **I'M NOT FAT, I'M JUST PREGNANT.**

SYLVIE: (*Offended.*) Hey, I'm not "fat," I'm just "pregnant…"

Now I know it probably doesn't matter to *you*, and I know it probably shouldn't matter to *me*, but – Certain people *think* things… And I don't want those people thinking their certain "things" about *me*…Because I'm not – This – I've worked hard for my shape…So to see that shape – Changing…Out of my control, out of my arena – out of my comfort zone…

Because I *do* have a comfort zone…(*Indicates belly.*) And this zone is not comfortable…If the food police were watching – I would get a ticket…A ticket in this area…It doesn't matter there's a baby in there…People can't tell yet, that there is a baby…It's not baby-*like*…It's just – There…

And people see it…People see me. (*She is embarrassed.*) People see *me*.

(*She skulks off. Blackout.*)

Scene 8: **CORN DOGS.**

> (*Lights rise on empty stage. Kertie sneaks onto it.
> She looks at audience. Then –*)

Corn dogs Hot dogs Cheese dogs Chili dogs

> (*Blackout. Rise.*)

Devil dogs.

> (*Blackout. Rise.*)

Suzy Q's.

> (*Blackout. Rise.*)

Anything Entenmann's.

> (*Blackout. Rise.*)

Everything *non*-Entenmann's.

> (*Blackout. Rise.*)

Anything with no pulse.

> (*Blackout. Rise.*)

No fat.

> (*Blackout. Rise. Explaining –*)

The stringy "white" fat…Not the "calorie" fat…

> (*Blackout. Rise.*)

"Low" calorie…is "yuck" calorie…It tastes like – "No" calorie…

> (*Blackout. Rise. Heavenly –*)

15

KERTIE (cont'd): Caloric…Caloric *in*take…

(*Blackout. Rise.*)

Twenty…Twenty five hundred.

(*Blackout. Rise.*)

In two days…

(*Light grows wider, not believing her.*)

Okay hours…

(*Grows wider, still not believing.*)

Minutes…!

(*The light fades – then stops, questioning. Kertie grows offended. The light continues to shine.*)

I don't have anything left!

(*She turns out her pockets, shows the light there is nothing. The light fades…then suddenly, fades back up again – not believing her.*

Kertie threatens it. It fades quickly – blackout.)

Scene 9: **MOMENT OF TRUTH.**

(Lights rise on Suzanne. She smooths the wedding veil on her head. She considers trying on her wedding gown.

She tries, has difficulty. Tries harder, has more difficulty.

She gets into it. It is really, really small and snug.

Blackout.

Lights rise on Renee. She jogs on stage, then stops, beginning to limp.

She examines her ankle.

She takes out a bandage, and wraps it.

She tries to walk. Her ankle still hurts.

She gets an idea.

She drops. Begins to do crunches.

Blackout.

Lights rise on Tara. She walks over to a garbage can. She throws gravy, mashed potatoes, sardines and sauerkraut in the can.

Kertie enters, and sees Tara.

Finished, Tara exits.

Kertie approaches the can. She lifts the lid, and looks in. Makes sure no one is looking. Then she reaches in the can, and takes out a handful of sauerkraut.

She eats it.

She reaches in for more as – blackout.)

Scene 10: **PIECE.**

> (*Jess begins her monologue, but seeing something – stops. Addressing Audience Member #2 –*)

JESS: Piece of it…I want a *piece* of it…If you would just give me a *piece*. Not a whole piece or half a piece – but just a little…

> (*House lights rise. Jess approaches Audience Member #2. Takes his/her slice of cake.*)

Yes, that's it…A little sliver…Then I could feel calmer…Then I could feel…"good…" Not good like when you do something you're supposed to do, because you know it is right, and you get this big warm fuzzy feeling but because –

> (*Eats.*)

Yes…YES…Because there are pleasures in life. Pleah-zures… And people should really enjoy those pleasures – before they die. Before they are **not able** to enjoy them anymore.

People have "lips," people have "mouths." God gave us these lips and mouths so we could do something *with* them. If we weren't supposed to *do* something, then he wouldn't have *given* them.

He gave us *stomachs*, too. Stomachs for collecting *food*. Some of us have bigger baskets than others. *Some* of us, are bigger gatherers. And there's nothing wrong with being a bigger gatherer. It just proves – It just proves – That we are *better* at it. We are better gatherers. We are *good* at something. Better than those skinny people. We don't need to be skinny people. Not when God is relying on us to do his work. To fill his baskets. The baskets that *he* made. (*Beat.*) If he didn't want us to have them, he wouldn't have *made* them. He wouldn't have made "food." He wouldn't have made "cake."

> (*Considers. Decides.*)

Why don't you just give me it all then…I mean, since it's there…I mean, God wouldn't want you to waste it.

19

(*Takes the rest of cake.*)

JESS (cont'd): You don't need it. Your basket is too small. You can't carry –

I can carry…I can carry that cake. I wear it well. *You* don't wear it at all.

We can't see it…So why bother?

(*Blackout.*)

Scene 11: **COKE.**

FRIEDA: "Real" Coke…Not any of that fake shit…Real caffeinated, one hundred and fifty calalories, sweet sweet sugary, Fun Dip on a Lick-A-Stick sippin' Coke…Because real women drink Coke…Real women don't – Sit around, waiting for their 'Perrier' to be delivered…No…Real women are – Going to the grocery store. Grabbin' it – because their kids want it. Demand it…

> (*Child enters, grabs onto Frieda's leg.*)

Real women don't have time to argue.

> (*She shakes Child off.*)

They don't have time to stand there trying to understand it. Trying to decipher – Between this and that. That and this. Real women don't have time to read the labels, much less understand the nutritional values – so I just keep it down to the basic core – Coke, or no Coke. Water, or no water. 'Cause sometimes I substitute water. Water, I know, *has* no calories. And water is free!

But sometimes, you need more than water. Sometimes, you need a kick.

> (*Kicks Child away.*)

To keep your kids in line. To handle your kids.

> (*She loses it.*)

And the alternative to Coke would be booze – and you don't want me imbibin' do ya…Not when I have a five year old, and a four year old, and two three month olds…

I need a kick…I get that kick outta Coke…(*Demanding, like an addict.*) So give it to me.

> (*A can of coke flies onstage. Frieda catches it. She opens it, chugs. Pause. She burps. Is satisfied. Crossfade.*)

Scene 12: **NUTS.**

> (*Chloe stands with a bag of nuts.*)

CHLOE: "Nuts…" You're bringing "nuts" into this house…!?
What are you – If not stupid…If not – Totally insane…These have
calories…! And I can't have these calories – Clogging up my
cabinets…!

> (*Stands there, hating him.*)

Get it out of here then…Get – It out…And while you're at it –You
get out of here, too.

You *know* I am on a diet…Didn't I tell you I am on a diet…? So I
don't want things like nuts – I don't need things like nuts – Sitting
here – Tempting me in this house!

Maybe you can control yourself – but I…? I can't, control myself…
I see these nuts – And I feel like a squirrel…Like a squirrel –
Foraging for the winter…A squirrel stuffing her cheeks – Until she
cannot stuff them anymore – *That* is how I feel. *That* is what I'll do
– So when you tempt me – You are just making it worse. You are
just making – An already bad situation worse.

> (*Considers.*)

So I can't have you around me. If you are not willing to respect my
boundaries –

And I don't care whose house it is. *You* pay the food bill…You
should be glad…! Glad that I am saving you so much money…
Because you don't have to buy things…Things like nuts…Which
can get expensive…

> (*She begins to explain.*)

So it all works out in the end. I save you money on "food," thus
saving money for the "house," you put this money toward the
"house," in the form of a "mortgage" bill – So really "I" am paying
for the mortgage…That's the way it is…

22

(*She urges him away.*)

CHLOE (cont'd): So you and your nuts – Get out of here…!

The door is closing. It's closed. (*Afterthought.*) And I'm locking the cabinets.

> (*We hear a murmur. Lights fade as* **APPLE, PEACHES, PUMPKIN PIE.** –)

Scene 13: **APPLE, PEACHES, PUMPKIN PIE.**

> (*Dark stage.*)

VOICES (HEADS): Apple peaches pumpkin pie/Feed the girls and make them cry/Apple peaches pumpkin, Gee/They can eat it, why can't we?

> (*Dream lighting fades up. Heads appear.*)

HEADS: Apple peaches pumpkin pie/Feed the girls and make them cry/Apple peaches pumpkin, Gee/They can eat it, why can't we?

> (*Chloe doesn't know what is happening.*)

Apple peaches pumpkin pie/Feed the girls and make them cry/Apple peaches pumpkin, Gee/They can eat it, why can't we?

> (*Devils move in – and whirl Chloe away.*)

Apple peaches pumpkin pie/Feed the girls and make them cry/Apple peaches pumpkin, Gee/They can eat it, why can't we?

> (*Kertie walks by, happily.*)

Apple peaches pumpkin pie/Feed the girls and make them cry/Apple peaches pumpkin, Gee/They can eat it, why can't we?

> (*Lights flash on disembodied heads.*)

Apple peaches pumpkin pie/Feed the girls and make them cry/Apple peaches pumpkin, Gee/They can eat it, why can't we?

> (*Howard Stern, Hugh Hefner and Donald Trump enter.*)

Apple peaches pumpkin pie/Feed the girls and make them cry/Apple peaches pumpkin, Gee/They can eat it, why can't we?

> (*Howard Stern, Hugh Hefner and Donald Trump rip off Kertie's clothes. She stands there, covered in fig leaves.*)

24

HEADS (cont'd): Apple peaches pumpkin pie/Feed the girls and make them cry/Apple peaches pumpkin, Gee/They can eat it, why can't we?

> (*A snake appears. Chloe fights her way onstage – but devils hold her back.*)

Apple peaches pumpkin pie/Feed the girls and make them cry/Apple peaches pumpkin, Gee/They can eat it, why can't we? Apple peaches pumpkin pie/Feed the girls and make them cry/Apple peaches pumpkin, Gee

> (*Chloe breaks through the men.*)

CHLOE: *They* can eat it.

HEADS: WHY CAN'T WE?!

> (*The snake hisses. The lights fade, slowly.*)

Scene 14: **SHUT UP.**

(*Stage is dark.*)

KELLI: Your voice…It's grating…So if you could *just not speak*…
Just not speak…for two seconds…

(*Two seconds pass. The lights rise, slowly.*)

The seconds have passed…The two seconds have passed…And I do
not hear you…You are *not* speaking…And I feel so much better
really I feel so much better…(*Puts hands over her ears.*) My ears –
Unburdened…My ears are now unburdened…Unloaded…Unloaded
with the loads you lay upon them…

Sorry…I guess I am sorry…But your voice…! And it's not so much
the "way" you say it, but the "things" you say. Do you ever think
about things before you say them…? Huh…? Do you ever
consider…being considerate…?

I do not have Big Legs…They are just – "Wider." "Wider" than
yours…Women have "bigger legs…" Women who don't run every
day like you run every day have bigger legs than you…We need
fat…For our babies…We require it. Require the fat…To insulate…

If you were a woman, you'd know…If you were a female… you'd
understand…

Don't tell me my legs are big…I know my legs are big…But you
don't get it…You don't…understand…

So I don't want to hear it…

Not from you – Not, from you.

(*Crossfade.*)

Scene 15: **I EAT BECAUSE II.**

TWO: I eat because I am sad

THREE: Because I am lonely

ONE: Because I need a friend

NINE: Food *is* my friend

SIX: Because no one is telling me *not* to eat

FOUR: Because someone is saying – "no. Don't eat it…" And so I

THREE: (*Spitefully.*) Bite the food

TWO: Chew the food

THREE: Chew the food

TWO: Tear the food –

FOUR: – I put it in my mouth

ONE: On my tongue

FOUR: I roll it around

NINE: Between my teeth

THREE: And then I

TWO: Scarf the food

ONE: Swallow the food

TWO: Swallow the food

ONE: Ingest the food –

SIX: – I put it on his bill

27

NINE: On his tab

SIX: I make him pay for –

> *(Stops, looks at her body. Realizes it is really she who is paying for it, in added weight.*
>
> *Lights rise on Felicia. She sits in a pile of "finished" food. She feels guilty.)*

SIX (cont'd): Then I *hate* the food

ONE: Curse the food

FOUR: Curse the food

TWO: Regret, the food…

> *(Felicia turns from audience. She begins to purge.)*

SIX: Then I

NINE: Hide the food

THREE: Trash the food

FOUR: Trash the food

NINE: Forget the food…

> *(They sit, miserable.)*

SIX: I sit and cry…

> *(The lights fade. A baby begins crying.)*

Scene 16: **GROWTH.**

(*Sylvie is more pregnant than before. The cry fades.*)

SYLVIE: The baby is coming…I can't exercise…Not enough…
Not enough to make a difference…And so I don't…And I continue
to grow, and grow…

Growth…is a good thing. Growth…Means there's something inside,
developing…Gestating…Forming its parts…Becoming whole…
When it comes out of me –

I will be changed…My body will be changed…My body will serve
a purpose…My breasts will serve a purpose…

(*Jenny crosses. She carries a bag.*)

I'll look at the young girls – without babies. Whose bodies have no
purpose. No meaningful purpose…

(*Jenny exits.*)

Why do they judge…How can they know…How can they possibly
know…

(*She looks at her belly. Miraculously –*)

A woman is born…Another woman…

(*Sylvie considers Felicia, who is exhausted from purging.
She suddenly grows worried for her unborn daughter.*

Blackout.)

END ACT I.

ACT II.

Scene 1: **CONSUMED.**

> (*Tara sits with a plate of food. The plate is on a black
> tablecloth. It appears to be suspended in darkness.*
>
> *Tara nods cordially to the " imaginary" diners at other
> tables. Then she begins to eat.*
>
> *She mixes the food together. Then picks it up with her
> fingers, and alternates leisurely between fingers/fork.*
>
> *She picks up the pace, forking in more mouthfuls.*
>
> *Then she shoves it in with her hands – grabbing a pie from
> under the table – and cookies and Diet soda.*
>
> *She takes a second plate of food from under the table and
> eats*
>
> *As*
>
> *Chloe stands with a Frito.*

LICK & SUCK.

> *Chloe licks the Frito, then sucks it.*
>
> *Finished, she puts it in her pocket.*
>
> *Then she takes out another. Repeats.*
>
> *Meanwhile*
>
> *Jenny sits with a bag. She takes string beans and peaches
> out of the bag.*
>
> *She gets a plastic baggie and cup from under her pillow.*
>
> *She places the baggie in the cup.*

31

She begins chewing string beans.

CHEW & SPIT.

Finished, Jenny spits the string beans in the cup.

She continues to chew & spit as

Kelli stares at a dinner roll.

Meanwhile

Tara gorges

Chloe licks/sucks

Jenny chews & spits

Tara finishes her meal. (*The actress playing Tara then sits there experiencing whatever she is experiencing. She does not throw up or purge – she is not a bulimic, just a normal, out-of-control eater).

Finished, she gathers herself and stacks her plates.

Then something – a breath? a sigh? A smile?

She places her knife and fork neatly on her plate.

Blackout.

Chloe sucks her last Frito. She places the Frito in her pocket and rolls the bag closed.

Blackout.

Jenny completes her last chew & spit. She seals the baggie of chewed/spit food closed, and places it under her pillow.

She sits back.

Blackout.

Kelli continues to stare at roll.

CONFUSED.

After a while, Kelli's resolve begins to waver. She looks at her body.

She takes out a sweatshirt, and puts it on.

She looks at roll.

She takes sweatpants out of her bag, and puts them on.

Looks at roll.

She continues to look at roll. Her mind begins to wander.

Her eyes come to rest on the arm of her sweatshirt. She notices there is some give in the sweatshirt. She is surprised. She dares to look for some give in the sweatpants – finds some.

Finally confident, she takes the roll, and places it firmly in her mouth.

She chews.

Gulps.

She looks at her empty plate.

She looks at her stomach.

She feels nothing.

Blackout.)

Scene 2: **SALAD.**

>*(Chorus passes a salad quickly down a line, as if in a game of "Hot Potato." The salad lands on Frieda.)*

FRIEDA: Salad…What am I gonna do with a salad…?!

>*(Chorus exits.*
>
>*Suzanne enters, wearing her too-small wedding dress. She is weary, in search of a salad.*
>
>*She sees salad, and grabs it from Frieda.*
>
>*Suzanne eats.*
>
>*Frieda steps backward.*
>
>*And eats.*
>
>*Frieda steps backward.*
>
>*And eats.*
>
>*Frieda exits.*
>
>*And eats.*
>
>*Blackout.*
>
>*And eats.*
>
>*Blackout.*
>
>*And eats.*
>
>*Blackout.*
>
>*And eats.*
>
>*Blackout.*

And eats. Grows bored.

Blackout.

And eats. Grows more bored.

Blackout.

And eats. Gets tired.

Blackout.

And eats, gets more tired.

Blackout.

Gets more tired.

Blackout.

Falls asleep.

She drops her head in the salad.

Blackout.)

Scene 3: **I DON'T FEEL GOOD.**

> (*The stage is dark. We hear the crackle of potato chip bags.*
>
> *Lights rise on empty bags/cans/boxes of diet and junk food.*
>
> *Lights rise on women. They are bloated and miserable. Hold. Then –*)

FELICIA: I don't *feel* good.

CHLOE: I don't *look* good.

RENEE: If I looked better, I wouldn't be eating this

KERTIE: Shit

CHLOE: Crap

> (*Anger builds within the group.*)

RENEE: FUCK.

KERTIE: It sucks…It really does suck.

> (*They linger, not knowing what to do.*)

CHLOE: And I don't want it to suck…I want it to be

FELICIA: Breezy

RENEE: Light

CHLOE: Like the girls in the magazine ads. Eating yogurt.

KERTIE: They are

FELICIA: Breezy

RENEE: Light

CHLOE: Without the calories

KERTIE: But aren't they

RENEE: Starving?

KERTIE: I mean I know *I* am

RENEE: Starving

KERTIE: And I don't want to

CHLOE: Deprive myself

KERTIE: God knows I wouldn't

RENEE: Deprive myself

KERTIE: I work hard

FELICIA: I am

(*Kertie stops. Thinks. Reaffirming –*)

KERTIE: "Hard-working…" And I deserve to be rewarded. I deserve to be

RENEE: Loved

KERTIE: In the only way I *can* be loved

CHLOE: With chocolate…(*Women fly in with candy boxes. Begin to imbibe.*) God made chocolate…And on the ninth day, he didn't say – Let me go on a diet…

JESS: He rested…God *rested*…

SYLVIE: That was on the eighth day.

JESS: The eighth?

SYLVIE: The day before he (presumably) *made* the chocolate.

CHLOE: He had to gear up for the chocolate.

JESS: So what of the "tenth" day. The day "after" the chocolate…

SYLVIE: He ate!

> (*Blackout.*)

Scene 4: **I EAT BECAUSE III.**

FIVE: I Eat

TWO: Because

THREE: Because

SEVEN: Because

FOUR: Because

EIGHT: Because –

FIVE: I am hungry.

> (*They consider.*)

TWO: No.

EIGHT: Nah.

SEVEN: I don't think so.

> (*Blackout.*)

Scene 5: **I EAT BECAUSE IV.**

(A director's slate slams: "TAKE 2")

FIVE: I eat because it's there

THREE: Because it's warm

FIVE: Because it feels good on my palm –

TWO: – in my hand –

EIGHT: – between my fingers –

FIVE: – I eat because it's expected

SEVEN: It's polite

FIVE: And refusing would be rude. I mean, how does one refuse?

TWO: Some tea

THREE: Some cake

FIVE: When you go over to an Italian mother's house

EIGHT: For dinner

SEVEN: For dessert

FIVE: I mean you *have*

TWO: To eat

FIVE: Because *not* eating would be

EIGHT: Not socializing

FIVE: And you want to socialize, don't you…I mean, you don't want to appear…"anti-social."

SEVEN: To be labeled –

TWO: Cold

THREE: Weird

> (*Suzanne cooks with a frying pan, Five assists.*)

FIVE: Not caring about a person's preparations…About the things they cook…Of being "high maintenance…"

THREE: Of being a vegetarian

TWO: Or a vegan

SEVEN: Of someone allergic to gluten

THREE: Of needing a special meal

EIGHT: Of eating a special diet

JESS: (*entering, overwhelmed*) Of LIVING a special *LIFE* –
Different from everyone else – Because you're –

I don't want to be special…I just want to be like everyone else…I want to eat like everyone else…The people on McDonald's commercials. Or Wendy's. The skinny people in magazines. For two for one buffets…Not "one" for two…Not one "eating" for two…

> (*A very pregnant Sylvie crosses. She eats something disgusting.*)

Although if I were *her* it wouldn't be so bad…Not half as bad as – The whole I can't get rid of…

> (*Renee jogs by.*)

I *could* get rid of…I *won't* get rid of…

> (*The group considers.*)

41

EIGHT: I don't have time

TWO: Money…

THREE: It's too intense…

SEVEN: It's like a full time job

TWO: And I have a full time job

EIGHT: I have kids

THREE: Pets…

FIVE: I have a husband…

SEVEN: I certainly don't have time for myself.

JESS: I could *make* time…I would have to…make time…

(*A clock ticks. Blackout.*)

Scene 6: **I WANT.**

SEVEN: I don't want time.

THREE: I don't need time.

EIGHT: I want…a chocolate-covered strawberry.

(*Seven sighs. Lights fade, slowly.*)

Scene 7: **BONES.**

JENNY: Food sticks…When you are washing it down with milkshakes, food sticks…It sticks to your ribs…And your hip bones…I never thought that I had a hip bone…But one time I was very sick. Very sick – and I saw…a hip bone…And a rib…Ribs that were so pronounced…That it made my father cry…It made *me* cry…to see my father crying…Because he never did cry you know. Even during the worst times. Times when – I don't know. He lost some money in the stock market. Or when his mother died. He didn't even cry when his mother died. But when he saw me…

>   (*She trails off. Continues.*)

Ribs…Sticking to ribs…The food sticks…Usually you can't *see* the ribs. When you eat. When you eat things like bread and milkshakes – (*protesting*) – things I don't want to eat, but I have to…Stuff I don't want to – Force inside…I don't want to force – But he's feeding me. My dad, is feeding me…I CAN'T eat it…I don't WANT to EAT it…It STICKS inside of me…It sticks to my RIBS…

>   (*Lifts up shirt. Shows torso.*)

You *SEE*…? You *SEE*…?

>   (*Pokes where ribcage should be.*)

You CAN'T see it…You can't see RIBS…

>   (*She is overcome. Brings down her shirt. Tries to comfort herself.*
>
>   *Lights fade.*)

44

Scene 8: **CRUEL TRICK.**

> (*Sherry stands in her underwear. There is a covered mirror nearby.*)

SHERRY: It's not me…I stand here by myself wondering to myself thinking to myself – is it really me…? Or just some cruel…"trick," perhaps…Some cruel trick – played out by the master of all cruel tricks…Someone who has devised this trick to personally torture and humiliate –

And what if it's not some cruel trick…What if I'm really here because of the things I did – The choices I made…Of deciding to eat this thing and that – Until I didn't realize how much I was eating – Until suddenly, I became this *thing* that I do not recognize.

> (*Drops cover. Examines herself in mirror.*)

I do not recognize that body in the mirror…Why it looks different to me. Why it looks different than the body I had growing up in high school. And then through college – It is **not** me…(*Turning to audience, panicking.*) Someone has done something wrong… Someone has *SAID* something –

I did not *think* these arms were too wide. I did not *conceive* that these pants could be – anything smaller, anything smaller than the size they are – I thought that designers were designing differently now. And that pants were being cut "smaller." I couldn't understand why pants were being designed smaller. It had to be the fashion. The *new* fashion – that I was missing out on. Because I was *older.* Because I had not *heard* about it. Because I didn't under*stand*! –

> (*Turns to mirror.*)

How could I not see it…How could I not look in the mirror and see…What everyone else was seeing…How could I not know…?

> (*Lights dim. Young Sherry appears in mirror.*)

Things get busy…Things get busy – and you don't find yourself looking in the mirror anymore. Not in that way. Not in the way you

SHERRY (cont'd): did when you were young. When you had to be pretty, and beautiful, to get someone...(*Considers.*) You meet someone...You think he loves you for who you are – He has sex with you – So there you are, thinking everything is fine...And then...And then...He turns you to the mirror...

(*Turns to mirror.*)

You look in...But you don't see – You look in – But you do not understand...

(*Sherry/Young Sherry step toward each other.*)

You step forward...Your face is dry...The lines by your eyes are wrinkled...

(*Young Sherry retreats.*)

You see age...You see maturity...

(*Sherry stands alone, horrified.*)

You see – You see.

(*Blackout.*)

Scene 9.

(IMAGES FLASH.

They are images of thin and fat things:

Barbie, thin celebrities, Miss America, Miss Universe, etc.

A cow, a pig, a hippopotamus, a whale, a bulldozer, a blimp, etc.

Magazine covers advertising diet & exercise strategies.

Renee Zellweger as a before-and-after "Bridget Jones."

Celebrities (like Star Jones and Carnie Wilson) "before" and "after" their weight loss surgeries.

A "fat" and then "thinner" and then "fat-again" Oprah.

Celebrities with eating disorders who are currently in the news.

Book covers for bestselling books "Flat Belly Diet," "The South Beach Diet: Supercharged," "You: On a Diet," "Skinny Bitch," "Skinny Bitch Bun in the Oven," etc.

A promo for the TV show, "The Biggest Loser."

Infomercials selling diet pills & exercise equipment.

Isagenix products.

Images flash quicker and quicker.

They stop.

Lights fade.)

Scene 10.

    (*The stage is dark.*)

REBECCA'S VOICE: Just because *you* don't believe it, doesn't mean I have to stand here and stop doing it…People have beliefs… Beliefs that may be different than yours…And you shouldn't make other people whose beliefs are different than yours try to change them…Change is not good…Not when it is forced by other people…As if they could force…As if they'd attempt – To force… Because you can't force someone…

    (*Lights rise on Mound.*)

You believe what you believe…

    (*The curtain comprising the Mound drops. Rebecca is revealed. She is obese, larger than life.*)

REBECCA: And I believe what I believe…Which is – Something you cannot just come up to me and change. "Change…?" Because you're trying to trick me? Because you're trying to brainwash me…? Because you're trying to make me be more like you? Because you don't "like" chocolate cake?

I "like" chocolate cake…And just because you think that a person like me shouldn't eat it – Just because *you* think, in your "thin" little head –

VISIONS.

I have vision…And in my visions, I see a person who is big, and fat, and beautiful…And most of all – happy…Happy because she is eating chocolate cake…And because she doesn't have to think about – The ugly things that *you*. That *you* see…When you see someone like me…eating chocolate cake…

    (*Rebecca approaches Kertie. Kertie swings cake away.*)

48

REBECCA (cont'd): When you force me, to see what you see... When you are so blind...that you can't see someone at all...Only "fat." Only "calories..." Sugar... Sweet, sweet sugar...Coating me...

(*Felicia enters, moving toward cake.*)

Making you – (*declining, losing her breath, having chest pains, realizing*) Hate...this cake...You hate...this cake, don't you...Don't you...Hate...to eat...Whatever...you like...Whatever...you want...

(*Kertie gives cake to Felicia.*)

You can eat it, you know...You can have it...You can have cake...

(*Kertie and Rebecca disappear. Thin Felicia considers cake.*)

ELEPHANT. (cont'd)

FELICIA: Not when I feel like...Not when I **am**...this Elephant myself.

(*Hold. She releases her grip, and lets the cake fall.*

Blackout.)

EPILOGUE.

(*The screen reads:*)

THE FACTS

(*Fade.*)

A 2008 survey by SELF magazine in partnership with the University of North Carolina shows that 6 in 10 women between the ages of 25 and 45 report having disordered eating behaviors.

(*Fade.*)

1 in 10 have symptoms consistent with full-blown eating disorders like anorexia and bulimia.

(*Fade.*)

The average American woman is 5'4" tall and weighs 140 pounds.

The average American model is 5'11" tall and weighs 117 pounds.

The average American model is 98% thinner than most women.

(*Fade.*)

(The women begin to assemble.)

80% of women say that the images of women on television and in movies, fashion magazines, and advertising, make them feel insecure.

(Fade.)

80% of women are dissatisfied with their appearance.

(*Fade.*)

Americans spend over $40 billion on dieting and diet related products each year...

>*(The women strike poses unique to their characters (For example, Renee does a downward dog, Sylvie holds her pregnant belly, etc.)*
>
>*All stand behind Felicia. Felicia is the anchor, and the characters appear to be different shades of Felicia.*
>
>*Felicia faces the audience, and offers them a slice of chocolate cake.*
>
>*The lights fade.*
>
>*Blackout.)*

END OF PLAY

QUESTIONNAIRE.

(The audience views completed questionnaires in the theater or lobby. The questionnaires are comprised of these questions:)

What is your favorite food?

What is your favorite dessert? How often do you eat dessert?

Would you consider yourself to be overweight?

Have you ever tried to lose weight? If so, what is the most extreme thing you have ever done to try to lose weight?

Have you ever made fun of someone for being overweight?

Are you happy with your body size?

Whom do you consider to have an ideal body?

How do you feel about healthy foods like salads and vegetables?

Are you male or female? What is your age?

Do you feel the need to be thin? If so, why?

(*If an audience member would like to fill out a questionnaire, they can do so. Their questionnaire can then be added to the display for the run of the production.

At the end of the run, the completed questionnaires may be mailed to the playwright, for incorporation into a larger work.

The questionnaires can list real, fake or anonymous names.)

Props.

Edible chocolate cake, small drinks, napkins or plates (for audience)
A gray cover (for the Mound)
Hand weight
Gigantic pile of food
A fake cooked crab
A fake piece of wedding cake
A plastic wedding cake topper
Can of Reddiwhip
A large bandage
Garbage can
Can of gravy
Box of mashed potatoes
Tin of sardines
Edible sauerkraut
An apple
Can of Coke
Bag of nuts
A small bag
3 plates
A black tablecloth
A table
A chair
Edible food
A pie
Cookies
Diet soda
A bag of Fritos
A plastic baggie
A cup
String beans
Peaches
A dinner roll
A knife
A fork
A pillow
A sweatshirt
A gym bag
A pair of sweatpants
An edible green salad

Props. (cont'd)

Potato chip bags
Bags/cans/boxes of diet food and junk food
Box of chocolates
Director's slate
Frying pan
Something disgusting and edible
A full length-mirror frame
A mirror cover
An edible piece of cake
Questionnaires
Pens & Pencils

Special Costumes.

A wedding veil
A wedding dress
Devil costumes (2)
Howard Stern costume
Hugh Hefner costume
Donald Trump costume
Fig leaf covering
Snake costume

Made in the USA
Middletown, DE
12 September 2016